What is the Meaning of the Numbers and Letters on Fishing Boats

This question Is often asked, so first l~~e~~ numbers or letters at all. The answer catch either fish, lobsters, crabs, scal **and** intending that their catch will be However before the owner or skipper of a boat can gain a fishing licence the boat must be *registered*. The letters and numbers issued on registration are displayed on the boat to show that the boat has indeed been registered, and provide a means of identification. You may immediately think of 'fishing boats' you have seen which do not have registration numbers. These are unlicensed boats and, as such, they are not permitted to catch fish for commercial purposes, and the quantities of the various fish which they may catch is very restricted and precisely stipulated, and there are severe penalties for infringement.

Even with a licence, fishing vessels are restricted both in where they can fish and what quantities they can catch (The QUOTA SYSTEM) in order to protect fish stocks for the future. The fishing industry is highly scrutinised and there are bodies such as the Royal Navy Fishery Patrols and local area Fishery Protection Bodies who have vessels which check on the fishing activities of boats in their area of influence. They have the authority to board any fishing vessel to check the logbooks, size of nets used, where they have been fishing and the size, type, and quantities of their catches. To do this they have to be able to recognise fishing vessels while at sea, and the system of letters and numbers is the means by which this is done.

To find out how the present registration system came about and what the letters mean it is necessary to look at the fascinating historical story, and this is told in the following pages.

At Newlyn

FISHERIES PATROL VESSELS & FPV PENNANT

At Teignmouth

HISTORICAL BACKGROUND

There has been some registration of commercial shipping since the 16th century and amongst historical archives there exists a 1572 'Register of English Merchant Ships and their Masters' compiled by Thomas Colshill, the Surveyor of the Port of London. A series of Navigation Acts from 1660 brought about the registration of ships with the intention of compelling British merchants to transport their goods in British built ships with British crews. This was to promote the British ship-building industry to ensure there were enough ships and competent crews for the Royal Navy in times of war.

Before the American War of Independence, British Colonies in the West Indies were supplied by ships from America. American independence meant that the trade with plantations in America was lost to Britain, but she had no intention of forfeiting the lucrative trade with the West Indian colonies. America on the other hand also badly needed this trade, and what was a former British Colony, was transformed into a dangerous rival. It was announced in 1783 by Lord Sheffield that it was the duty of the British Government to discourage and crush American Navigation. With this in mind a system of general registration of British vessels was introduced with the Navigation Act of 1786. Ship-owners were then required to register all vessels of more than 15 tons burden with the customs officer in their home port This included the larger fishing vessels. Each certificate of registry was numbered and entered into a registration book, and transcripts were sent to the central registry at the Custom Houses in London and Edinburgh. The record included:-

- Port registry number, and date and place of registration
- Vessel's name and home port
- Names of masters and occupations and addresses of owners
- Place, nationality, and date of construction, or capture as prize
- Type of vessel, tonnage, number of decks and masts, hold depth and (somewhat curiously) whether it had a gallery or figure head.

The registration number was carved into the main structural beam of the vessel, but not displayed externally.

Customs officers had been involved in the registration of ships since 1701, and following the 1786 Act, the Registrar General of Shipping was established under the Board of Customs. An 1854 Shipping Act transferred the responsibility for all matters relating to merchant ships, but not fishing boats, to the Board of Trade, and for the purpose of registration, fishing boats were not considered separately from general commercial shipping until 1854. The involvement of HM Customs ceased only in 1986.

IINTRODUCTION of FISHING VESSEL LETTERS & NUMBERS

The idea of fishing vessels displaying an identifying number unofficially started in about 1820.   At that time following the end of the war against France, there was still considerable friction between French and English fishing vessels.   There was also an extensive smuggling trade taking place from both the continent and the Channel Islands, to England and Ireland, (in which many fishing vessels were heavily involved, particularly when fishing was poor).   To enable French and British officials of the respective Navies and Customs to recognise and identify fishing vessels a reciprocal agreement was made with France that all fishing vessels, as well as having an official number, should display the first and last letters of their home port followed by an identifying number.   In the UK this was formalised by a Sea Fisheries Act (SFA) of 1843.   The task of allocating the port letters and numbers was given to the HM Customs officers since they already had the task of general shipping registration, so the registration ports were those which had a Custom House and they were not necessarily the ports from which the most fishing took place. The vessel's official registration number was still carved internally.

The system of using the first and last letters raised some anomalies however, as ports like PortsmoutH and PlymoutH, GuernseY and GrimsbY, PoolE and PenzancE had the same first and last letters.   In 1868 a further SFA sorted out some of these anomalies which resulted in for example, Penzance taking the letters 'PZ', Portsmouth a single letter 'P', and Guernsey the letters 'GU'.   Most registration ports tried to follow the pattern of having the first and last letters of the port, but three ports in Scotland - Buckie (BCK), Broadford (BRD) and Inverness (INS), and South Shields (SSS) in England were allocated three letter designations.   These exceptions were made at the discretion of the local Customs Officers who originally allocated them, in order to avoid any confusion with other ports round the UK.   A few ports such as Anstruther (AR) were about to be allocated Port Letters but the Custom House closed before the scheme was finalised and they were never allocated.   The list of fishing registration ports and their 'Port Letters' was detailed in a Merchant Shipping Act of 1894, and reissued unchanged in a 1993 Act.   The 1894 Act required every fishing boat to be lettered and numbered, to have official papers, a registration number, and be entered on a register.   It also laid down the minimum age for crew as 16, though apprentices could start aged 13.   Annual returns were made from each port, which were recorded as the series 'Statistical Register of Fishing Vessels'.   The overall length of the boats, registered tonnage, port number, official number, engine power, fish catch capacity, date and nationality of build, and the hull construction material are now listed.   The early registers included details of the type of fishing boat and how many crew, but these details are no longer listed. Figurehead's are also no longer considered worth listing! (see p2). Several ports on the West Coast and

Outer Islands of Scotland had no Customs Officers, and the task of issuing registrations was given to the local Fisheries Officers. Though most of the old Custom Houses are no longer used as government offices, they can usually still be found, and they were often impressive buildings as illustrated.

FISHING VESSEL CLASSES

Fishing vessels were initially divided into two classes. A 1st class boat was over fifteen registered tons and displayed the Port Letters before the number. 2nd class boats were sailing vessels under fifteen registered tons and displayed the numbers before the Port Letters. 3rd class boats - essentially rowing vessels - were added later, and like the 1st class boats, had the letters before the number, with the size and lack of masts differentiating between them. Individual Customs officers often had their own ideas about allocating the numbers. For example, St Ives boats were numbered numerically such that a 1st class vessel might have SS1, a 2nd class 2SS, and a 3rd class SS3, while the Penzance officers numbered each class numerically so that one could have PZ1, 1PZ and PZ1 again for a 3rd class vessel. The St Ives Customs officers applied another of their own systems for the numbers by allocating

150PZ—2nd Class Fishing Vessel

the numbers 1 to 500 for boats located both in St Ives and ports to the west of it, such as Sennen Cove, and numbers above 500 to boats in ports the other side of St Ives such as Hayle. The Port Letter Numbers of boats in this area, while not adhering strictly to this policy, still show this old pattern.

As steam vessels were introduced in the 1870s, there was understandable indignation on the part of their proud owners when these, then 'state of the art' vessels, were classified as 2nd Class, since the machinery space reduced the vessels fish carrying capacity, and therefore the registered tonnage to below 15 tons. To redress this bone of contention, steam vessels were thereafter allowed to use gross tonnage. (In simple terms the gross tonnage is the total volume of a vessel's enclosed spaces where 1 ton equals 100 cubic feet (or 2.83 cubic metres), and the registered tonnage is the same but minus the volume of the engine compartment and the crews quarters.) The Scottish ports came under the control of the Fishing Board of Scotland based in Edinburgh, and they had a slightly different method of calculating the registered tonnage and defining how the boats fell into the three different classes, with the length of keel playing a major part in the calculation as well as the breadth, draught and shape of hull. The division of boats into three classes ceased following a Sea Fisheries Act of 1903.

FROM CUSTOMS TO CARDIFF

In 1986, the RSS (Register of Seamen and Shipping) in Cardiff took over from HM Customs the task of issuing fishing vessel registrations and Port Letter Numbers, which then became known as **PLN**s. The numbers have generally been issued in sequence but there is now a trend to reissue the lower numbers provided that the older boats which had gained the lower numbers have been retired or scrapped. In some ports a higher number than the next in sequence was granted by special request, and subsequent number allocations issued in sequence. This has resulted in whole series of numbers never being allocated at all. However, If owners wish to acquire a special number, or reuse an old number, they have to be able to prove that the old number has been out of use for a minimum of five years, unless the change is that of one owner changing his old number to a new boat. There is considerable superstition in the fishing industry and in some places it is considered lucky to have a number in which the digits add up to ten, such as 64, 91, 730, or just 10. As well as requesting a special number, owners may also request to use a different port of registration from their local port.

The numbers and letters have to be painted on the sides of the hull at bow and stern as high as possible, and should strictly be either black letters on a white background or white letters on a black background. Since Merchant Shipping Acts of 1894, 1988 and 1993, the size and thickness of the lettering has been laid down with an increased size required in vessels of length greater than 17 metres. The numbers and letters must also be displayed on part of the structure facing upwards, so as to

PLN on Vessel >17m

be visible from the air, and in a contrasting colour to the background. The vessel's Name and Port of Registration must also be clearly displayed on the stern of the boat in letters of eight centimetres in height. This

Name & Registration Port on Stern

contrasts with most private boats which usually display

PZ481   1. On Hull
2. Vertically Upwards
3. On Lifebelt

the port from which the boat operates. Both the vessel's name and the PLN must also be displayed on the lifebelts. Should a vessel be unfortunate enough to sink, the lifebelt would probably remain afloat to identify the lost vessel and indicate its last position. It is possible however to see many variations in satisfying these requirements, and the inspecting officers who now come from the surveying branch of the MCA - (Maritime & Coastguard Agency) have some degree of discretion over a vessel's markings, especially with smaller vessels, where to display all such markings would be impractical. The important priority is that the PLN markings are such that the vessel can easily be identified at sea from any angle. The official registration number is still carved into the main structural beam of the vessel.

In the days of sail, the PLN had to be displayed on the mainsail, in a contrasting colour to the sail, as well as on either side of the bow. When sails were no longer used, the requirement came in for the PLN to be painted on both sides of the hull near the stern as well as on the bow. Many modern boats however, still carry a small mizzen sail on the mizzen mast near the

DS2 on the MAINSAIL

stern of the vessel for stability and keeping the bow into wind, and the PLN will often be seen on the mizzen sail. Following the increased fuel costs there may well be a return to the use of sails to augment the engine power, particularly when in transit to and from the fishing grounds, and we may see more of the PLNs imprinted on the sails.

For full details of marking required, see Appendix on Page 16

SC53 on the Mizzen

PORT OF REGISTRATION AND OPERATING PORT

The Port of Registration is frequently not the port from which the fishing vessel operates, as several ports in one area may come under a single port of registration. Also as a boat gets bought and sold, the PLN and registration, and the fishing licence, are often sold with it, and the boat continues under its old registration at the port of the new owner. Many owners prefer to keep a shorter number of the old port rather than re-register with a longer number at the new one. The cost of repainting the numbers in five locations on the hull adds significantly to the cost of re-registration. Some just feel it is unlucky to change the number! This explains why so many boats operating from a port, (as well as those just visiting it), can be seen displaying Port Letters other than the local port of registration. Indeed they may have a registration from a port at the other end of the country. As an aside, many TV viewers watching the series 'Doc Martin', which was filmed in Port Isaac, thought that the boats in harbour with Port Letters 'PW' (from nearby PadstoW) were registered in the fictional 'Port Wenn'!!

When boats cease working, the number should be removed, or painted out, but it is still possible to find the old PLNs on boats which are no longer in use as commercial fishing boats, and the owners having not yet complied with this regulation.

LI247—Crossed through

HERITAGE BOATS

It is understandable that owners of heritage boats might wish to keep their original registration to lend authenticity to their appearance although no longer fishing. Sometimes such historical fishing vessels can be seen with a thin red diagonal line through the PLN, as shown on the accompanying picture, to indicate that the vessel is no longer officially registered. This followed a suggestion by one of the registrars, but it is not official policy.

PRESENT POLICY

Any fisherman wishing to operate from a particular port will now request a PLN, in order to register his vessel, from the RSS (Register of Shipping and Seamen) in Cardiff. The registration costs something in the region of £110. They can then obtain a licence from the Fisheries Officer at the local Regional Administrative Centre for the type of fishing they wish to carry out. Only vessels under 10 metres length that either fish for salmon or eels, or boats that have no engine fitted, are exempt from having a licence.   Many boats under ten metres registered length have a general licence, but the larger boats need a licence for each particular type of fishing.   This licence cost can be a significant outlay of up to £35,000 even for a small craft, and considerably more for the larger craft.   The engine(s) power output and VCU (Vessel Capacity Unit) or fish carrying capacity, both have significant influence on the licence cost.   If a fishing licence is not obtained within six months of registration, the registration is then cancelled.   The penalties for fishing without a licence were laid down in the 1894 Act at £20 with forfeiture of the boat, but are now as much as £50,000 with possible forfeiture of the catch, the fishing gear and even the boat.

On the following pages are alphabetical lists (by the 'Port Letters') of the fishing registration ports in the UK with two maps showing their locations.   Since fishing vessels from Southern Ireland are often seen in UK ports there is also a list of the Irish registration ports.   About eight of the ports on the following lists are no longer used for fishing and do not have any boats registered, and a dozen or so more have very few boats operating, with some having only one.   Some of the ports of registration still have boats on their registers even though very little, or even no, fishing activity continues from the ports.   Truro (TO), Bristol (BL), Carlisle (CL), Manchester (MR) and Runcorn (RN) for example have no fishing activity, but still register a few boats.   Fowey (FY) and Penzance (PZ) on the other hand, although having very large registered fleets, have very few boats operating from them.   To a lesser extent, some others such as Inverness (INS), Kirkaldy (KY), Leith (LH) and London (LO) mostly cover other ports in their local areas.   The ports which no longer have any, or few, boats registered are shown in the 'Comments' columns in the following lists   Dutch fishing boats have a similar registration scheme and one Dutch port in particular causes some confusion. The Port of **UrK** has the Port Letters (UK)!!

Recent Portland (PO) PLN

RECENT ADDITION
After the Royal Navy left Portland in 1996 the new Port Harbour Authorities asked the Register Office in Cardiff for Portland to be made a General Shipping Registration Port, which was actioned by a 1998 amendment to the Shipping Act of 1993.   Cardiff then offered Portland the choice of also becoming a Fishing Registration Port, which was taken up, and actioned by an amendment in 1999, allocating '**PO**' as the Port Letters. This was the first addition to the list for over 100 years. Since 2004 a few small boats have been allocated the 'PO' designation.

ALPHABETICAL LIST of REGISTRATION PORTS in UK

Port Letters	PORT	LOCATION	COMMENTS
A	Aberdeen	Eastern Scotland	Major fishing port
AA	Alloa	Near Stirling	Not in Use
AB	Aberystwyth	West Wales	
AD	Ardrossan	SW of Glasgow	
AH	Arbroath	NE of Dundee	
AR	Ayr	S of Prestwick	Mainly Spanish Boats!
B	Belfast	Northern Ireland	Major Port
BA	Ballantrae	SW Scotland	
BCK	Buckie	East of Elgin	
BD	Bideford	North Devon	For Appledore & Clovelly
BE	Barnstaple	North Devon	A few small boats Reg
BF	Banff	Between Buckie & Fraserburgh	
BH	Blyth	N of Newcastle	
BK	Berwick on Tweed	N tip of E England	
BL	Bristol		No Fishing
BM	Brixham	South Devon	Major Port
BN	Boston	The Wash	
BO	Bo'ness	E of Edinburgh	
BR	Bridgewater	Severn Estuary	No fishing. Few boats Reg
BRD	Broadford	Isle of Skye	
BS	Beaumaris	Anglesey, N Wales	
BU	Burntisland	N of Edinburgh	Not in Use
BW	Barrow in Furness	NW England	
CA	Cardigan	W Wales	
CE	Coleraine	Northern Ireland	
CF	Cardiff	South Wales	
CH	Chester	River Dee	No Large boats Reg

Port letters	PORT	LOCATION	COMMENTS
CK	Colchester	NE of London	
CL	Carlisle		No fishing. Few boats Reg
CN	Campbelltown	Sth Kintyre	Major Port
CO	Caernarvon	N Wales	
CS	Cowes	Isle of Wight	No large boats
CT	Castletown	Isle of Man	No fishing. Few boats Reg
CY	Castlebay	Sth Outer Hebrides	Major Port
DE	Dundee	Eastern Scotland	No large boats
DH	Dartmouth	South Devon	
DO	Douglas	Isle of Man	No fishing Few boats Reg
DR	Dover	SE England	No large boats
DS	Dumfries	N of Solway Firth	No fishing
E	Exeter	South Devon	For Exmouth & Local area
F	Faversham	N Kent	
FD	Fleetwood	N of Blackpool	
FE	Folkestone	Kent	Kent & E Sussex Ports
FH	Falmouth	South Cornwall	Major Reg Port for area
FR	Fraserburgh	NE Scotland	Major Port
FY	Fowey	South Cornwall	Major Reg port,
GE	Goole	East Yorkshire	Not in Use
GH	Grangemouth	Near Edinburgh	No fishing. Few boats Reg
GK	Greenock	Near Glasgow	Little fishing. Few boats Reg
GN	Granton	Near Edinburgh	Not in Use
GR	Gloucester	River Severn	Not in Use
GU	Guernsey	Channel Islands	Major Port
GW	Glasgow		Not in Use
GY	Grimsby	Lincolnshire	Major Port
H	Hull	River Humber	Major Port

Port letters	PORT	LOCATION	COMMENTS
HH	Harwich	East Anglia	
HL	Hartlepool	N of Middlesborough	
IE	Irvine	N of Prestwick	No fishing. Few boats Reg
IH	Ipswich	East Anglia	Local ports
INS	Inverness		No fishing, Major Reg Port
J	Jersey	Channel Islands	
K	Kirkwall	Orkney Islands	Major Port
KY	Kirkaldy	South Fife Coast	Pittenweem & Fife ports
LA	Llanelli	West of Swansea	Small craft only
LH	Leith	Edinburgh	Major Port
LI	Littlehampton	Sussex	W Sussex ports, small craft
LK	Lerwick	Shetland Islands	Major Port
LL	Liverpool		No large boats
LN	Kings Lynn	The Wash, Norfolk	
LO	London		Thames Estuary ports
LT	Lowestoft	S of Gt Yarmouth	Major Port
LY	Londonderry	Northern Ireland	Not in Use
M	Milford Haven	SW Wales	Major Port & local ports
ME	Montrose	NE of Dundee	
MH	Middlesborough		N Yorkshire Ports
ML	Methil	South Fife	
MN	Maldon	Essex	
MR	Manchester		No fishing. Few boats Reg
MT	Maryport	NW of Keswick	
N	Newry	Northern Ireland	Major Port
NT	Newport	Gwent, East of Cardiff	No fishing. Few boats Reg
OB	Oban	West Scotland	Major Reg port for W Coast
P	Portsmouth	Hampshire	No Large boats

Port letters	PORT	LOCATION	COMMENTS
PD	Peterhead	North of Aberdeen	Major Port
PE	Poole	Dorset	
PH	Plymouth	South Devon	Major Port
PL	Peel	Isle of Man	
PO	Portland	Near Weymouth	Few boats Registered
PT	Port Talbot	East of Swansea	Few boats Registered
PW	Padstow	North Cornwall	Major Port & local boats
PZ	Penzance	Nr Newlyn, S Cornwall	Major Reg port. No fishing
R	Ramsgate	Kent	
RO	Rothesay	R Clyde Estuary	
RR	Rochester	Kent	
RU	Runcorn	Manchester Ship Canal	No fishing. Few boats Reg
RX	Rye	East Sussex	Major Reg port Kent & Sx
RY	Ramsey	Isle of Man	Little fishing. Few boats Reg
SA	Swansea	South Wales	
SC	Scilly	Isles of Scilly	
SD	Sunderland	S of Newcastle	
SE	Salcombe	South Devon	
SH	Scarborough	East Yorkshire	East Yorkshire Ports
SM	Shoreham	Sussex	West Sussex Ports
SN	North Shields	South of Newcastle	
SR	Stranraer	SW Scotland	Few Boats Reg
SS	St Ives	North Cornwall	Hayle & Sennen
SSS	South Shields	South of Newcastle	
ST	Stockton	Stockton on Tees	No fishing. Few boats Reg
SU	Southampton	Hampshire	
SY	Stornaway	Outer Hebrides	Major Port
TH	Teignmouth	South Devon	

Port letters	PORT	LOCATION	COMMENTS
TN	Troon	South of Glasgow	
TO	Truro	South Cornwall	No fishing. Few boats Reg
TT	Tarbert	Loch Fyne	
UL	Ullapool	NW Scotland	
WH	Weymouth	Dorset	Weymouth & Dorset Ports
WI	Wisbech	Norfolk	Not in Use
WK	Wick	NE Scotland	Wick & local Ports
WN	Wigtown	South West Scotland	No fishing Few Boats Reg
WO	Workington	West of Keswick	
WY	Whitby	North Yorkshire	Major Port
YH	Great Yarmouth	East Anglia	

PORTS OF REGISTRY in SOUTHERN IRELAND (EIRE)

Port letters	PORT	LOCATION	COMMENTS
BA	Balina	NW Ireland	
C	Cork	South Ireland	
D	Dublin		Major Port
DA	Drogheda	South of Dublin	Major Port
DK	Dundalk	North of Dublin	
G	Galway	West of Ireland	
L	Limerick	River Shannon	
NS	Newry	South East Ireland	
S	Skibbereen	South West Ireland	Major Port
SO	Sligo	North West Ireland	Major Port
T	Tralee	South West Ireland	
W	Waterford	South East Ireland	
WD	Wexford	South East Ireland	Major Port
WT	Westport	Western Irreland	
Y	Youghal	East of Cork	

LOCATION of FISHING REGISTRY PORTS in ENGLAND, WALES, NORTHERN IRELAND and EASTERN EIRE

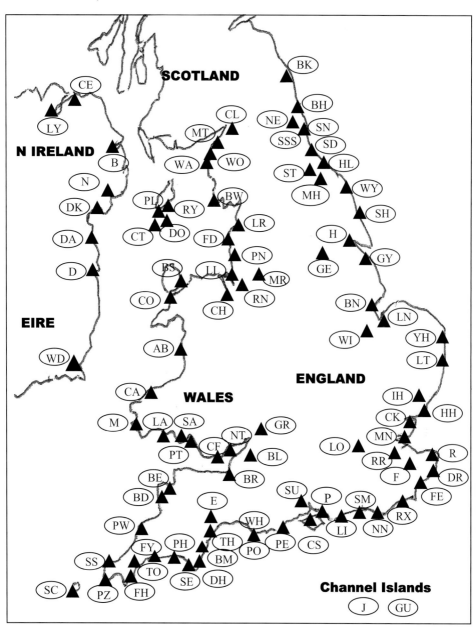

NOTE   **SSS & NS** Co-located
                      WH & PO Co-located

LOCATION of FISHING REGISTRY PORTS IN SCOTLAND
including the ORKNEY and SHETLAND ISLANDS

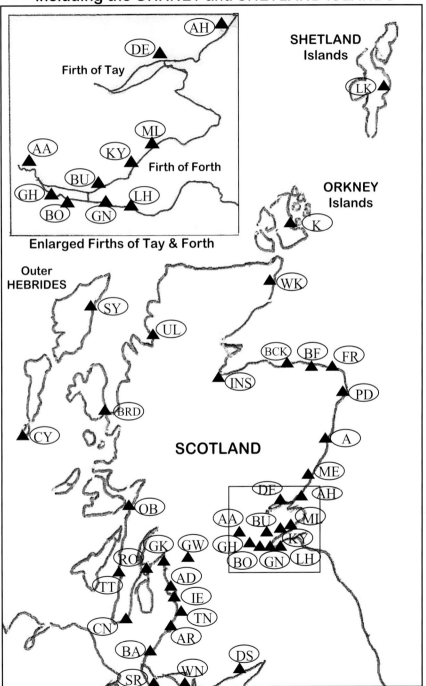

APPENDIX

EXTRACT FROM THE MERCHANT SHIPPING (Registration of Ships) REGULATIONS OF 1993

A fishing vessel is to be marked as follows:-

(a) The name of the vessel and the port of choice shall be painted in white on a black background or in black on a white background outside the stern of the boat in letters which shall not be less than 8 centimetres in height, and 1.5 centimetres in breadth, and

(b) the port letters and the number of the vessel shall be painted or displayed on both sides of the bow and on each quarter, as high above the water as possible so as to be clearly visible from the sea and the air, in white on a black background or black on a white background;

(c) For vessels; not over 17 metres in length, the height of the port letters and number shall be at least 25 centimetres with a line thickness of at least 4 centimetres;

(d) For vessels over 17 metres in length, the height of the letters and numbers shall be at least 45 centimetres with a line thickness of at least 6 centimetres;

(e) The port letters and numbers shall in addition be painted or displayed on the wheelhouse top or some other prominent horizontal surface;

(f) The vessel's official number shall be carved into the main beam of the vessel or, if that is not possible, marked or fixed thereon in the manner prescribed.